THE HERO'S GUIDEBOOK

THE HERO'S GUIDEBOOK

CREATING YOUR OWN HERO'S JOURNEY

WRITTEN AND ILLUSTRATED BY ZACHARY HAMBY
EDITED BY RACHEL HAMBY

DEDICATION

For Rachel, my perfect partner in everything, and Luke and Jane. May you always be heroes.

Roads go ever ever on
Under cloud and under star,
Yet feet that wandering have gone
Turn at last to home afar.

ISBN 978-0-9827049-7-4

The Hero's Guidebook: Creating Your Own Hero's Journey
Written and Illustrated by Zachary Hamby
Edited by Rachel Hamby
Published by Creative English Teacher Press in the United States of America

TABLE OF CONTENTS

INTRODUCTION

You are about to begin a secret look at what makes hero stories so exciting and inspirational—sort of a road map to the path that most heroes follow. As this journey unfolds, I will use example characters and situations from many books and movies. Some of these are classic stories like *The Hobbit* by J.R.R. Tolkien and *The Wizard of Oz* by L. Frank Baum. Others are newer stories like *Harry Potter* and *Star Wars,* and several are animated films like *The Little Mermaid, Aladdin,* and *The Lion King.* I even use tales from Greek mythology, Norse mythology, legends of King Arthur and Robin Hood, and modern superheroes like Superman, Batman, and Spider-Man as examples. Whew! There sure are a lot of hero stories!

When choosing which stories to include, I tried to pick ones with which most readers would be familiar. But even if you are not familiar with a particular book or movie, don't worry. I will give you enough of the details so you can still understand the example. As you read along, I'll also encourage you to think of a hero story that's special to you. You might be surprised what you find hidden within it! The journey awaits!

THE POWER OF HERO STORIES

Have you ever noticed that people love stories about heroes? Movies about Batman, Superman, Wonder Woman, and Spider-Man pack the theaters. Books that take readers to far-off lands and let them experience epic quests are bestsellers. Even popular video games give players a chance to control a heroic character. This love of heroes isn't just a phenomenon in our culture either. Hero stories are popular all over the world—and all throughout history, too. People 3,000 years ago liked hero stories just as much as we do—maybe even more so. So what is it about hero stories that make them so timelessly beloved?

Exciting, far-off places might have something to do with it. We like hero stories because they transport us out of the real world. Taking out the garbage, babysitting your little sister, studying for the math test—sometimes you just have to escape. Hero stories take you to new and exciting places full of creatures and adventures that you could never see in real life. (I'm still waiting to see a real-life hippogriff, but it just hasn't happened yet.) In stories you see heroes completing mighty, impossible-looking quests that you secretly wish you could be a part of. Since hero stories are so different from real life, they allow us to escape from our real-life problems, and we all need that every once in a while (even we adults).

We also love hero stories because of what they can teach us about real life. You may think: I don't buy it. I don't have superpowers. I've never pulled a sword out of a stone. All of these statements are true, but stories are sneaky. While you may be experiencing imaginary adventures, you're learning real-life lessons. By being there with heroes as they face their struggles and seeing how they react to their problems, stories teach us how we should act when we come up against our own obstacles. You may never literally slay a dragon or defeat a supervillain, but you will encounter your own problems, which will seem just as terrifying and impossible.

Two of the greatest storytellers of all-time, J.R.R. Tolkien, author of *The Hobbit* and *The Lord of the Rings,* and C.S. Lewis, author of *The Chronicles of Narnia,* said that stories have a special power—a healing power. It's easy for us to get caught up in the struggles of everyday life. We see our problems piling up, and we forget that there is hope and help available to us. But when we enter the imaginary world of a story, it's like we are healed of a sickness. The attitude of the story's hero reminds us that we need to have courage, too. The hero's problem of saving the whole world makes our real-life problems seem smaller. We remember to hope. Imaginary stories help us see the true reality of life again. Coming back from the story world, we can see the real world in a new, inspired way. Lewis said that in stories "we do not retreat from reality; we rediscover it." It's no coincidence that the common message in a lot of famous hero stories is having hope in even the darkest of times. In stories obstacles are never as impossible as they seem. All giants can fall, and all dragons have a weak spot. If that theme of hope can spill over into real life, it can change everything.

Just like many hero stories have a similar message, they also have a similar hero-story pattern. The Hero's Journey (or monomyth) is a story-pattern first made famous by a scholar named Joseph Campbell. He discovered that hero stories from all over the world had many of the same stages and characters. This was an exciting discovery because hero stories come from vastly different times and places. How was it possible that they could be so similar? Well, since stories are a reflection of real life, the human experience is universal. Underneath our superficial differences, we are all human. We have the same hopes, dreams, and fears, and these are reflected in our stories.

Because the Hero's Journey is rooted in the human experience, its storytelling pattern can also serve as a way of looking at life. In history books you will find many real-life heroes who have done amazing deeds. In a way they went on their own hero quests. Their accomplishments required just as much bravery and sacrifice from them as the heroes you find in storybooks. In fact, their life-stories even have some of the same stages as a hero's journey. This is because the pattern of the Hero's Journey is also the pattern of life.

This book will serve three purposes. First, it will help you understand how the ancient pattern of the Hero's Journey works, so you can develop a deeper appreciation for hero stories—not just those you already enjoy, but also those that you are going to enjoy in the future. Secondly, it will ask you to think about how the Hero's Journey can apply to your own life. How can you be a real-life hero? Hero stories can give you a fresh perspective on reality and your role in the world. Heroes are world-changers, and you can be, too. Thirdly, it will encourage you to create your own hero story. It's not only *reading* stories that makes us better people; it's writing them as well. As you read along, look for tips for creating your own hero quests.

A new journey is about to begin—one that I hope will help you re-discover what it means to be a hero and see the world through fresh eyes.

THE HERO'S JOURNEY

Way back in the fifth grade I was given the opportunity to write a story—any kind of story I wanted—and submit it for a contest. So, naturally, I chose to write a hero story. It was an eight-page epic about a boy who lives in a kingdom that has a gigantic wall all the way around it. Nobody in the kingdom has ever heard of magic or seen magical creatures. They have never thought about there being a wider world beyond their kingdom. Yet one day this boy, who just so happens to live in an orphanage, is visited by a strange, pointy-eared man who tells him the shocking truth: There *is* a whole world beyond the wall—a world filled with magic and magical creatures—and even more startling: It is the boy's destiny to journey there! As it turns out, the orphaned boy is actually the son of the King of the Elves, whose own kingdom is in mortal danger.

To make a short story even shorter, the boy goes through the wall, leaves the kingdom, and finds adventure. Along the way there are wolves and dragons to fight and princesses to rescue, and it all ends up nicely—and quickly. It was only eight pages long after all.

I'm not mentioning this because I think that it is a great story. (It really isn't.) I'm mentioning it because the story I wrote actually fit the ancient storytelling pattern called the Hero's Journey. Turns out, I had *accidentally* followed a pattern that is thousands of years old. All I knew is that I liked hero stories and wanted to write one. Since I had read other hero stories like *The Hobbit* and *The Lord of the Rings,* I had subconsciously followed the pattern of those stories. My hero began in an ordinary place, discovered that he had a secret destiny, took advice from a wise mentor, followed the path to adventure, and eventually saved the day. And what was the title of that middle school masterpiece that I wrote? *The Journey.*

Journeys play an important part in hero stories. Some journeys are more obvious than others. Some heroes literally travel miles and miles along a dangerous road. Other heroes go on journeys that are harder to see; they're emotional journeys brought about by a series of adventures that test the heroes. On the outside the heroes may not literally go far, but on the inside they have to dig deeper into who they are and what they believe. It's a journey of the soul. That's deep, isn't it?

Although Joseph Campbell discovered the story-pattern of the Hero's Journey and made it famous with his book *The Hero with a Thousand Faces,* he did not invent it. Over thousands of years storytellers from all over the world subconsciously used many of the same stages in their stories (kind of like I had done in my story). Sometimes the stages appear in a different order, or a few might be missing, but the general hero-story structure is the same. The common pattern is striking—and meaningful. Since we are all human beings, our stories reflect our lives in many of the same ways.

In our modern world the Hero's Journey still appears everywhere—not only in books, but also in movies, comic books, and video games. It shows up anywhere hero stories are told. The time and place of these hero stories may be completely different from one another: One may be set in space and another in a fantasy world of talking caterpillars and Mad Hatters. The stories might even take place in the modern world. This doesn't matter though. Heroes will follow the same pattern laid out in the Hero's Journey. It's fun to spot it in all different types of stories.

Rather than having you stumble onto the pattern of the Hero's Journey by accident (like I did), this book is going to make the pattern plain to you. This is not so you can simply copy it. The pattern will show you the building blocks of a good hero story. Then you can rearrange them however you want and build your own.

Hero stories are also filled with certain types of characters: The hero, the mentor, the ally, the shadow—just to name a few. These are called **archetypes** or character-types that show up time and time again in stories. This book will outline each of the important Hero's Journey archetypes for you as well. Many times these archetypes are actual characters in the story, but they can also be viewed as different masks that characters wear at different times. In fact, one character could be multiple archetypes in a single story—depending on what role that character is playing in the story at the moment. This may seem confusing at first, but it will become clearer over the course of the book. I want you be able to understand the Hero's Journey because it will help you understand *why* we human beings like hero stories so much: We need stories to show us the hero within all of us. These stories can help us in our own real-life journeys.

Then by adopting the Hero's Journey as your own, you can adapt it to any story you want to tell. This will keep the storytelling tradition alive for the next generation. The journey continues!

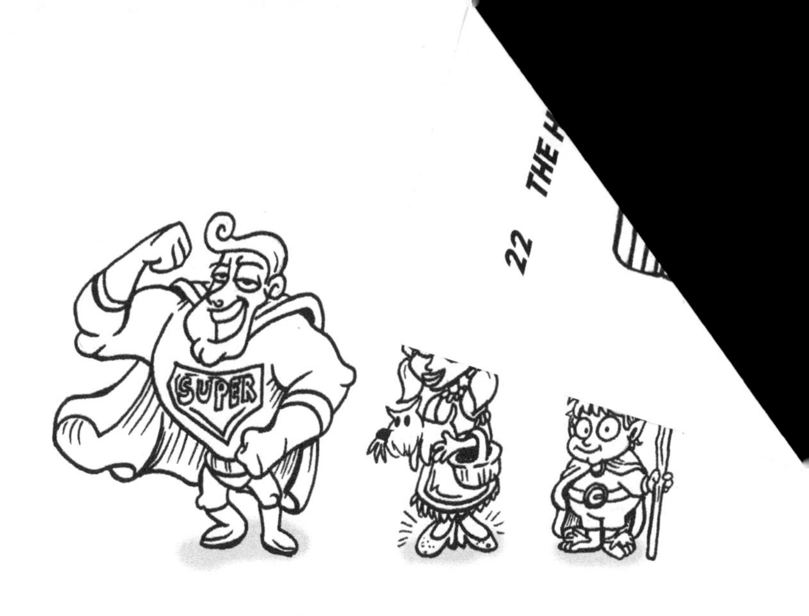

THE HERO

When you think of a hero, you might think of someone who is big and strong—maybe a man or a woman in a spandex costume or a flowing cape. But heroes don't have to be the tallest, the strongest, or the smartest people around. (Actually they don't even have to be people at all.) Heroes come in all different shapes and sizes. Some of the greatest heroes of all time have been people (or creatures) that no one would ever expect to do great things. *The Hobbit* is an epic fantasy adventure with a four-foot-tall hobbit as the hero of its story—not the type of hero you would expect as the main

character of a dangerous quest. But, as one of the characters in that story's sequel *The Lord of the Rings* puts it, "Even the smallest person can change the course of history." There is no height requirement for heroes—or any physical requirements really. Tall or short, strong or weak, male or female—none of these limit a hero. Not even age is a problem. Dorothy Gale from *The Wizard of Oz* is a young girl, and Carl Frederickson from the movie *Up!* is an old man, but they are both the hero of their own story.

On the outside heroes can be vastly different from one another, but on the inside most heroes are pretty similar. That's because heroes all have a code of right and wrong that guides them. Heroes do the right thing—even when nobody is looking. They sacrifice themselves for the good of others. In fact, we like to read about heroes because they remind us that there is still good in the world, and it's worth fighting for.

Choosing to fight on the side of good is a choice, which means being a hero is a choice, too. A hero is more than the main character of a story. The main characters' actions, how they choose to act, show us that they are truly heroes. As Batman says, "It's not who we are underneath, but what we do that defines us." When the world is in crisis, heroes choose to act—even when it means they must put themselves in danger.

Remember how heroes have something inside that motivates them into action—their inner creed, their code of right and wrong? I call this their **Hero Code**. In the legends of King Arthur his knights, the Knights of the Round Table, swore an oath—promising to defend the poor and weak. In the presence of their king they raised their swords and swore to heaven to uphold it—even unto death. It was this code that they lived (and died) by that allowed them to keep their kingdom safe.

In some stories it may take the heroes a while to listen to that Hero Code inside of them. It may literally be Jiminy Cricket who's trying to tell them to do the right thing or simply their inner conscience nagging them. These heroes spend a lot of the story running from what they know to be right, and only at the end do they shape up and become the hero they are meant to be. A good example of this is Simba in *The Lion King,* who spends much of his story being prideful, fearful, and unwilling to act. In the end he learns what it means to be a hero, and by watching his transformation, we learn how to act heroic, too!

Gilgamesh (yes, that's a person's name) is the main character of one of the world's oldest hero stories, *The Epic of Gilgamesh.* This story is so old that it was found chiseled out on a huge rock in an unknown alphabet. When archeologists finally translated it, they realized that it was an ancient hero story! In the story Gilgamesh, who has powers like an ancient superhero,

spends most of his time acting like a selfish brat—stealing from others because he's stronger and richer than they are. But since these actions aren't heroic, the gods sent him on an epic quest—a journey that teaches him a valuable lesson: He isn't the center of the universe. It cuts Gilgamesh down to size until he finally learns to listen to his Hero Code.

Heroes aren't perfect. Nor should they be. If heroes never made mistakes or had problems, we wouldn't be able to relate to them. One of the reasons the superhero Spider-Man is so popular is that when he's not out web-slinging and defeating super villains, he's an average, nerdy teenager with average, nerdy teenager problems. He's a hero though because in spite of all his shortcomings, he tries to do his best for others.

Some heroes' decisions make them lose the hero path along the way. Theseus, the ancient Greek hero who killed the half-man, half-bull

monster called the Minotaur, chose to leave a princess named Ariadne abandoned on an island while he sailed away. (She had just helped him defeat the Minotaur, by the way.) His hero story shows us that when heroes stop being heroic, when they go against their code of conduct, they also stop being heroes.

Not all heroes come from made-up stories. Real life has heroes, too—men and women who make the world a better place—and their lives are worth studying, but the heroes you find in stories are interesting because they were *created*. An author (just like you) first imagined them. They are "living" examples of characteristics that the author admired—things like bravery, loyalty, compassion, or honor. The author thought of these important qualities and then created a character that could represent them or act them out. The story gives the hero a chance to act out these qualities, and the audience has more of a chance to learn about them. People can *tell* you what it means to be heroic all day, but it's so much more exciting (and meaningful) when they *show* you through a story.

- As you read through the chapters of this book, think of your favorite hero story. (It might be a book, movie, or a video game.) Each chapter will ask you to analyze characters and events from that story. Try to use the same story each time, so you can see how the Hero's Journey pattern really does fit most stories!
- Think of your favorite hero story. Who is the hero of that story?
- What qualities make the main character a hero? (What are some of the things that character believes in? What is that character's Hero Code? What are some heroic deeds that character does?)
- Does the hero have any weaknesses? Do these weaknesses make the hero a more interesting character?

YOUR JOURNEY The reason we enjoy stories about heroes is that they inspire us and give us hope. They remind us that evil can be conquered if we face it boldly. They help us become better people. It might surprise you to hear that real life is like a story, too, and you are the hero of that story. But, like heroes, simply being the main character doesn't make you heroic. It's your choices—those inspired by *your* Hero Code, your sense of right and wrong—that will make you heroic!

Think about your Hero Code. What do you believe about right and wrong? How will this code drive your actions? You aren't perfect—just like heroes aren't perfect—but you can still choose to do the right thing…even when no one is looking.

WRITING TIP When you set out to design a hero for your story, you don't have to decide every detail about this character before you begin. Some writers begin by thinking of what kind of story they want to tell, and then they create a hero to fit their story. Other times writers create their hero first, and then think of what kind of adventure would fit that hero best. Either way, heroes and their stories go hand-in-hand. Just know that the qualities you give to your hero are those that you believe are the most important. Anyone who reads your story will see what you believe. It just happens!

Although heroes are characters we can look up to, they can't be perfect. Why? The audience can't relate to characters that don't have any weaknesses or problems. Think about Superman. Even though he can outrun a train, leap over tall buildings in a single bound, and withstand bullets, he still has one weakness: Kryptonite. That weakness makes him vulnerable and interesting. Heroes need to be able to make mistakes (and often they do). Otherwise, they might not be believable. However, good heroes learn from their mistakes and become stronger.

TYPES OF HEROES Remember how hero stories have been around for thousands of years? Well, during those years certain hero motifs have emerged within the larger pattern of the Hero's Journey. Below is a list of these common hero characteristics.

- **MISSING PARENTS** Many heroes are missing a mother, a father, or both. Sometimes heroes don't know the true identity of their parents (until this secret is told later in the story). For example, King Arthur begins life as a foster-child who has no idea he is truly the son of the King of England. In the film *Bambi* Bambi loses his mother early in his life. Later he learns that his father is the King of the Forest. This secret royal heritage makes the story more exciting.

OUTCASTS Some heroes have to live away from everyone else in society because they are different. Superman may have superpowers, but he's actually an alien from a planet that no longer exists. Talk about an outcast! Sometimes heroes are sent into exile in punishment for a crime that is not their fault. For example, Robin Hood must live in Sherwood Forest because he is choosing to fight against Prince John of England and the Sheriff of Nottingham. In *The Lion King* Simba runs away from the Pride Lands because he thinks that he caused his father's death.

PROPHECY In some stories the heroes have prophecies (or future predictions) made about them. This helps the heroes know that they have great things in store for them. For example, in the *Harry Potter* series there is a prophecy that Harry Potter is destined to destroy Lord Voldemort, an evil wizard. (Whoops! I shouldn't have said his name...)

- **ANTIHEROES** Some main characters in a story are not very heroic. They don't always make the best decisions and aren't good role models. They may not have much of a Hero Code, or if they do, they don't listen to it very well. For this reason they are called antiheroes instead of heroes. This doesn't mean they are villains. Usually antiheroes end up redeeming themselves by making a final good decision that helps make up for all their bad decisions.

- Can you think of heroes who fit these descriptions?

THE ORDINARY WORLD

Ordinary means "plain" or even "boring." The place where heroes live at the beginning of their story is called **The Ordinary World.** Dorothy is a little girl who goes on an amazing adventure to the Wonderful Land of Oz, a place full of talking scarecrows, cowardly lions, and winged monkeys. But her journey doesn't begin in Oz; it begins on the flat plains of Kansas, a place that is completely ordinary. Just like Dorothy, Superman, an amazing superhero, grows up on a farm—also in Kansas. (What is it about Kansas and heroes?) Most of us can understand why these heroes find a dusty farm in Kansas to be ordinary. (No offense to anyone who might happen to live on one.)

While the hero's home seems ordinary to him or her, it doesn't always seem ordinary to us. Sometimes it's just the opposite. For example, in *The Hobbit* the hero Bilbo Baggins lives in the Shire—a place where short, little, hairy-footed creatures called hobbits live in underground homes. That might seem like a fascinating place to us, but for the hobbits, it's completely ordinary.

Because their homes are so ordinary to them, a lot of heroes dream of visiting some other place. An example of this is Ariel in *The Little Mermaid,* who dreams of journeying to land, out of the sea. We might wonder, "Why does she want to leave? She's a mermaid who gets to be the daughter of the sea king, live in an underwater castle made of coral, and have a talking crab as her music teacher.

What's boring about that?" To her all the everyday things of land-living—things we take for granted like forks (dinglehoppers)—are more interesting. Her desire for adventure leads to her journey.

This desire to visit far off places is typical in a lot of heroes, but not always. Let's go back to *The Hobbit*. Bilbo Baggins has absolutely no desire to leave his hobbitty home. He's more of a sit-by-the-fire-and-not-go-on-adventures kind of guy. So it is shocking when an old guy with a beard (actually a wizard named Gandalf) shows up to tell Bilbo that he's about to be the hero of a new adventure. Even though Bilbo doesn't consider himself a hero, it turns out that he is just the guy (or hobbit) for the job.

A lot of heroes feel out of place in their ordinary world. They just don't belong for some reason. Sometimes this is a physical difference. Tarzan is raised by apes in the jungle, and he struggles with the fact that he does not look like the other apes. Sometimes the desire for adventure sets heroes apart. In *Star Wars* teenager Luke Skywalker can't wait to get off the desert planet of Tatooine, where he lives on a dusty farm (not exactly Kansas, but pretty close). Maybe the heroes have a special power that separates them from the other people who live there. In the Disney film *Hercules* the young hero has an unfortunate ability to destroy entire buildings with his super strength. This makes all the people in his small town shun and mock him. Yet all the things that make the heroes feel out of place are exactly the things that are going to help them succeed on their journeys.

Some heroes are born into an ordinary world that is hostile or abusive to them. Think about Cinderella, who is tormented by her evil stepmother and stepsisters. Her only friends are mice! And what about Harry Potter? He is forced to live under the stairs by his cruel aunt and uncle. Nobody would blame these heroes for dreaming of leaving the Ordinary World. When they receive the chance to escape these bad conditions—whether by an invitation to a ball or an invitation to Hogwarts—we rejoice with them!

Although many heroes are eager to leave the Ordinary World behind, as they adventure to far-off places, their opinion of their ordinary home begins to change. They start to miss the simple life it provided them. Places like the Land of Oz are fun to visit, but as Dorothy from Kansas says, "There's no place like home."

- Think about one of your favorite stories: What is the Ordinary World in which the hero begins?
- Does the hero enjoy living there? Does the hero desire adventure elsewhere? Or is the hero content to stay at home?
- How do the other citizens of the Ordinary World treat the hero?

YOUR JOURNEY Although you might like the place where you live, it may not seem very exciting to you—maybe even "ordinary." If you live in the countryside, you might think meeting someone who lives in the city is really interesting. You might ask a city person all kinds of things about life in the city, but turns out, that person is more interested about finding out about your life in the country. He or she might think you're the one who has the fascinating life. The grass is always greener on the other side.

Some heroes live in a place where there are few good things. Even from the time they are born, they have struggles to overcome. Your life may be like that, but remember: This is only a starting point. Your journey does not have to end here. The choices you make, just like a hero in a story, will guide where your story ends up.

The world is wide and filled with all kinds of adventure, but the place where we begin shapes us more than we realize. Whether your Ordinary World is good or bad, it is the first step in your own journey of life.

WRITING TIP At the beginning of your story, you might want to place your hero in a situation or place that he or she wants to escape. When designing your Ordinary World, you might want to consider where you want your hero to go. Usually the adventurous world that heroes journey into and the Ordinary World where they begin are vastly different. You can design the two worlds in a way that will contrast one another.

THE CALL TO ADVENTURE

If heroes chose to stay home instead of going on their adventures, both they *and the story* would go nowhere. No journey; no story. Instead we have books and books filled with exciting quests and dangerous missions. In every hero story there has to be a reason for the heroes to leave the Ordinary World behind. Leaving their home is often a frightening decision for them. How would you feel if you had to leave behind everything and everyone you've ever known? (Maybe you've had to face that yourself.) Plus, for most heroes there's the added danger that they won't come back alive. To get the story going, *something* has to happen. This "something" is named **The Call to Adventure,** an event that begins the hero's adventure. Sometimes it's a threat to the hero's home that suddenly appears: Robots invade the hero's planet or a deadly sickness starts spreading throughout all the people of the hero's village. These events spur the heroes into action.

Other times the Call to Adventure is delivered by another character called the **herald**. A herald is someone who delivers a message. In *The Hobbit* an old wizard named Gandalf shows up with twelve dwarves. Their mission? Recruit Bilbo Baggins, a fussy non-heroic hobbit to go with them to retrieve their gold that has been stolen away by a cranky dragon. In the film *Aladdin* a creepy, old man (really the villain Jafar in disguise) offers Aladdin a chance to gain large amounts of treasure by going into the Cave of Wonders. This opportunity, which Aladdin takes, leads him to a magical lamp, and the rest is history.

Technically, the herald doesn't have to be a character. It could just be an event in the story. In *The Wizard of Oz* a tornado whisks Dorothy away from Kansas to the magical Land of Oz. She has no choice to accept or refuse the Call to Adventure. The tornado forces her on the adventure of a lifetime.

Just like a phone call, the Call to Adventure can be answered or refused. Sometimes heroes try to refuse the call. The heroes might feel like they're not worthy, or they might just be scared. Who wouldn't be? But this attempt to refuse the job they were meant to do doesn't go well. They are heroes after all. In *Star Wars* at first Luke Skywalker doesn't want to go on an adventure with Obi-Wan Kenobi, a wise old Jedi knight. Luke works on his aunt and uncle's farm, and there's a lot of work to be done. So he refuses Obi-Wan's quest. It's only later, after a bit of tragedy, that he accepts the quest.

This part of a hero quest is called **Refusing the Call** because the hero initially rejects the quest. Ultimately, something in the story forces heroes back onto the heroic path. Heroes can't avoid their destinies. Maybe an event leaves them no other choice but to accept the quest. Or maybe they begin to think of what will happen if they *don't* accept the quest. Remember: Real heroes think of others before themselves. Eventually their Hero Code inside wins out, and they (reluctantly) accept the quest.

- Can you think of a hero who tried to avoid a quest?
- How did this work out for him or her?
- Why would it be hard for a hero to refuse a quest?

YOUR JOURNEY Life will present you with opportunities for adventure. Some you choose, and others you don't. Sometimes life forces you down a path that you do not want to take, but you must face it all the same. Refusing the adventures that life presents us with can leave us feeling dissatisfied. We must be willing to face our fears in order to make the world a better place.

WRITING TIP The hero that you create may be ready for an adventure—or maybe not. Heroes aren't always brave at the beginning of the journey. Giving your hero room to grow along the way is important. Think about how your hero might change on the adventure. What lesson will your hero learn? Maybe you can't answer that question just yet, and that's okay. Just send them on the quest and see what happens. As many authors have said, "The tale grew in the telling."

MEETING WITH THE MENTOR

Who is three foot tall, green, wise, and pointy-eared? A mentor! Even the greatest heroes need training before they can undertake their quests. That's why the next stage of the Hero's Journey is called **Meeting with the Mentor.**

The word *mentor* is a reference to an ancient hero story called the *Odyssey*. In this Greek myth a man named Odysseus is the main character, but his son, Telemachus (you can call him "Telly") is one of the heroes, too. When his father goes missing after the Trojan War, Telemachus is raised and instructed by one of his father's friends, a man named Mentor. So in reference that character's name, all trainers since then have been called mentors.

Mentors arrive in hero stories at just the right time. The **mentor** is an older and wiser character that gives assistance to the hero. Sometimes the mentor literally raises the hero, who has been orphaned for some reason. Other times the mentor appears when the hero has already accepted a quest but has no idea how to complete it. Other times, it's the mentor who gives the quest to the hero in the first place. Either way, the hero always needs the Yoda-like wisdom or training of the mentor to succeed on the quest.

Some people jokingly refer to this mentor as "the wise, old man" because so many mentors from old stories fit that description. King Arthur (before he earned the "King" part of his name by pulling a magical sword out of a stone) was mentored by Merlin, who trained him to become a good ruler. Merlin is a wise, old man who just so happened to be a wizard as well.

Obi-Wan Kenobi, the Jedi knight who trains Luke Skywalker in *Star Wars* is that, too: a wise old man. In *The Lion King* Simba is mentored by a wise, old baboon. (That's a little different at least.) Just because this is the mentor tradition, doesn't mean it can't be tweaked or modified. In the film *Pocahontas* the Native American princess Pocahontas receives wisdom from Grandmother Willow, a wise, old tree. Pinocchio receives wisdom from a cricket. Wisdom can be found in many different places, and mentors can fit many different descriptions.

Sometimes mentors have supernatural abilities like the use of magic or the power of the Force in *Star Wars.* Sometimes mentors can grant wishes—like the Genie from *Aladdin* or the Fairy Godmother from *Cinderella.* Sometimes they are hero-trainers who can instruct heroes in the art of adventuring (maybe using a sword, a wand, or a lightsaber). Sometimes mentors are just normal people who give wise advice, which proves just as valuable. In an interesting twist, some mentors are actually former heroes, who went on their own adventures long ago. Now they are passing the lessons they learned on to the next generation.

The training that mentors provide changes from story to story. In the film *Hercules* the Greek hero receives his training from a satyr (half-man, half-goat) named Phil. In the original Greek myth Hercules was trained by a centaur (half-man, half horse). The movie got it half-right! In both stories the lessons that Hercules learns from his mentor enable him to complete his mission.

Unheeded advice is worthless though. It's important that heroes listen to the advice that their mentors give them. If you've ever read the *Harry Potter* novels, you will notice that the lessons Harry and his friends learn in school (from their mentors) end up helping them later in the story. (I hate to tell you this, but that's how real-life school is supposed to work, too.) Preparation early in the journey will result in success later on.

Heroes should always choose their mentors wisely though. A **dark mentor** is an older character who appears to have the hero's best interest in mind but tries to lead the hero astray. The heroes don't realize that these mentors are actually evil, and they foolishly listen to their advice. An example would be Ursula the sea witch from *The Little Mermaid,* who seems to be helping Ariel by turning her human, but in reality she is merely using Ariel for her own plans. In Norse mythology the hero Sigurd is raised by a dwarf named Regin, who is only using the boy to slay a mighty dragon. Then once the dragon is slain, the dwarf tries to kill the boy as well. Luckily, the heroes usually realize what these dark mentors are up to before it's too late. Then the mentor shifts into a different type of character: the shadow (more on that later). As Mother Gothel, the woman who raises Rapunzel in the film *Tangled,* says as she shifts from a dark mentor to a full-fledged shadow, "You want me to be the bad guy? Fine. Now I'm the bad guy."

- Can you think of a mentor from a hero story you know well?
- How did the mentor help the hero?
- Can you think of a dark mentor from a hero story?

YOUR JOURNEY The neat thing about mentors is that they pop up in real life, too. Letting an adult be a part of your life is important. Your mentor might not literally be a gray-bearded wizard, but most mentors have wisdom from their own real-life adventures. (*Wizard* comes from the word *wisdom* by the way.) Mentors can share this wisdom with you and help guide you in the right direction.

Beware of dark mentors though. A mentor should be wiser than you—not just older. Adults who act the same age as you will probably not make the best mentors. Choose someone whom you respect for making good choices.

It's important to listen when mentors are

speaking. Their words of wisdom can save you from making mistakes. Just like in hero stories, their advice at this stage of life will equip you to face the challenges you will encounter later on.

WRITING TIP Mentors are vital to a hero's success, so make sure your hero has one. Who is an older and wiser person who could give your hero some important assistance? Will that person have special powers? Your story's mentor doesn't have to be "a wise, old man." Be creative. Try to find a way to make the old pattern new again.

THE TALISMAN

Heroes have their internal Hero Code that guides their actions, and they have their mentor who provides them with training, but they also require special tools or abilities in order to be successful on their quest. This is where the talisman comes in. The term *talisman* literally means an item with magical powers, maybe something like an amulet or a medallion.

In a hero story, the **talisman** is any kind of object, ability, or training that heroes receive to help them on their journey. Take any video game you have played recently: Think of all the special items there are to collect. These might be keys or swords or shields or other power-ups. Each one helps the hero be successful on the mission. That's what talismans do.

Sometimes the mentor literally gives the talisman item to the hero: The mentor hands the hero a lightsaber, a ring of invisibility, or a pair of ruby slippers. These talisman objects are easy to spot: King Arthur receives the mighty sword Excalibur from the outstretched hand of the Lady of the Lake. But other times the talisman is not an object at all, but a character trait that the hero already has: a superpower like flying ability or super strength, or a personality trait like courage or true love. In *Frozen* Anna is the hero of the story, and her talisman is her unconditional love for her sister, which allows her to complete her quest. In every case having the talisman will allow the hero to be successful. Whether the talisman is an object or a special skill, it usually falls to the mentor to help the hero use the talisman effectively.

In the ancient Greek myth of Perseus, a young man named Perseus accepts the "impossible" quest of defeating Medusa, a snake-haired woman who can turn anyone who looks at her into stone. Right after this, Perseus is visited by two gods, Athena and Hermes. These two mentors give him exactly what he will need to defeat Medusa: a cap of invisibility, flying sandals, a sword, a mirror-like shield, and a magical satchel to transport Medusa's head once he cuts it off. Just like in this story, the talismans that heroes receive perfectly match the task ahead and give them confidence that they can succeed.

As a more modern example, Batman is a superhero with no super powers. It might seem like he has no talisman. However, his talismans are the many gadgets that he uses to fight crime—the Batmobile, the Bat-rope, and the Bat-arang. Without these items, he would not be able to defeat his enemies.

The talisman can also present a danger to the hero. The item or ability gives the hero power, but it does not guarantee that the hero will always use it for good. As Spider-Man learned, "With great power comes great responsibility." Heroes are heroic because they use their power to help others, not themselves. In fact, a lot of villains are heroes who let their power go their head, and they turned to the dark side. (More on that later.)

Power itself does not make a hero; it is the choices that heroes make in the use of their talismans that ultimately determine if they are heroic. In the film *Aladdin* for much of the film the hero struggles with selfishness—using the power of the magic lamp to get only what he wants. It isn't until the end of the film when he decides to use the power of the lamp to set the genie free—a completely unselfish act—that he becomes a full-fledged hero.

Some talismans are so powerful that they cannot be used for good at all. The ring of power from *The Hobbit* and *The Lord of the Rings* is an excellent example of this. The ring begins innocently enough when Bilbo the hobbit finds it. It's just a magic ring that can turn anyone invisible. Who wouldn't want a ring like that? But then the characters slowly learn that the ring is completely evil. It has the powers of a dark lord trapped within it, and no matter how good your intentions are, it will eventually corrupt whoever wears it. The message: Too much power is never good.

The evil ring is a great reminder of the dangers that accompany having too much power. Think about it yourself: If you had the power to turn invisible, how would you use it? You might walk right out of school in the middle of the day. If no one could catch you, you might decide to do things that you knew weren't right. But this is what separates heroes from villains. Heroes do the right thing even when no one is watching. They follow their Hero Code. They always strive to use their powers for good and not let power corrupt them.

The dangers of too much power were why many ancient hero stories had unhappy endings.

In ancient Greece many hero stories ended with heroes succumbing to the lure of power. In the first part of the story the hero would accomplish amazing things through his mighty power—only to use that same power for selfish reasons and cause his own downfall. It is a warning that heroes of all ages must heed: If you misuse your power, you become your own worst enemy.

- Can you think of an example of a special item or ability that a hero receives in a story you know well?
- Can you think of a story where the talisman was not an object but a character trait instead?
- Did the hero require special training in order to use the item or ability well?
- Did the mentor assist the hero during this process?

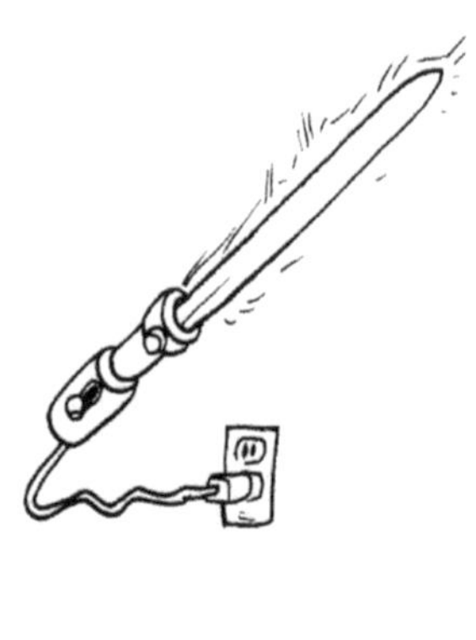

YOUR JOURNEY

You might not feel like you have many talents, but nothing could be further from the truth. We all have special abilities that are ours alone. A good mentor can help you find the skills that you have and help you succeed on your own journey. Training, which we call education, can also help you develop these skills, so you can be successful in the journey of life. Also remember not to let your power corrupt you. Once you realize what your special skills are, keep a level head and remain humble. Use these skills to better others first and not just yourself. In the end this will make you much happier.

WRITING TIP Once you know the quest you have laid out for your hero, think about what skills he or she will need to be successful. Will your hero need a special item? A special power? How can the mentor help train your hero for the journey ahead? Will the talisman tempt your hero to misuse it in some way?

ENTERING THE UNKNOWN: CROSSING THE THRESHOLD

A threshold is an area between two places. Doors have thresholds. Buildings have thresholds. Even life has thresholds. Taking the first step into a new venture is called "crossing the threshold," and that's why the next stage of the Hero's Journey, **Entering the Unknown**, also carries that nickname. In this stage the hero moves from the Ordinary World into a new unknown world.

Moving from a place that you know well into a place that is different can be both exciting and frightening at the same time. If you move to a new school, you might be excited to think of all the new people you will meet, but more often than not, you might be more frightened thinking about all the changes that lie ahead.

As brave as they are, heroes are no different: Braving the unknown is a big step for them, too. In their stories heroes must pass from a world that is usually safe and familiar into one that is strange and unfamiliar. It may not necessarily be frightening (at first), but the new world is usually filled with sights the heroes are not used to seeing. The first time Dorothy Gale steps out of her house (after a tornado has blown it all the way to Oz), she is in for quite a shock. Leaving her black-and-white world behind, she steps through across the farmhouse door threshold into a world filled with vibrant colors and huge flowers—not to mention munchkins. Oz is a dazzling place, but Dorothy soon learns it's also home to crazy things like winged monkeys and a wicked witch, who wants to kill her for her shoes. (Talk about some messed-up motives!)

Choosing to take that first step into a new place isn't automatic for heroes. Fear of the unknown often makes them pause on the threshold. Should they enter the new world? There is always the temptation to turn back. But if the heroes do not take the first step out of their comfort zone, they will never experience the adventure that has been prepared for them. Their journey will be over before it begins.

Giving up is exactly what the antagonists (the "bad guys" of the story) want the heroes to do. Their hope is that the heroes will see all the obstacles placed in front of them and decide *not* to save the day. The first obstacle that heroes meet is called a **threshold guardian.** This is a small-time obstacle that confronts heroes as they are just starting their adventure. It might be a monster that the heroes have to fight. It might be some other obstacle or problem placed in their way. If the hero is a cowboy, it might be a cattle stampede, or if the hero is a superhero, maybe a runaway subway train. It might even be the hero's own fear, which might be the most powerful threshold guardian of all. Even brave adventurers like Indiana Jones have a crippling fear. His is a fear of snakes. And guess what he often finds in the temples he explores? You guessed it. Tons and tons of snakes. Like all heroes he must face his fear.

Whatever form threshold guardians take, it is necessary for heroes to confront this challenge, overcome it, and move past it, so they can continue on their journey. Ultimately, the defeat of the threshold guardian makes the hero stronger.

Sometimes the threshold guardian is a character who is willing to join the hero's quest after seeing the hero's bravery and skill. For example, in the film *Tangled,* early in her adventure Rapunzel must enter *The Snuggly Duckling* inn, a place filled with violent, hooks-for-hands ruffians. This is a point where she might consider turning back and abandoning her adventure, but she perseveres. What she finds, after facing down the thugs, is that they are not really as mean and nasty as they seem. Just like her, they've got dreams! These "low-lifes" become some of her greatest allies.

Facing the threshold guardian is one of the hero's many chances of turning back and forsaking the journey, but as the hero will learn, each obstacle that is conquered builds courage for the next.

- Can you think of a threshold guardian in a hero story you know well?
- Can you think of a hero who had to face "fear" as his or her threshold guardian?

YOUR JOURNEY Trying new things is difficult. Getting out of our comfort zone is not a fun experience, but when we push past the fear, the uncertainty, and the doubting, that is when we find the things in life that truly excite us. To paraphrase Joseph Campbell: The cave you fear to enter holds the treasure you seek. So the next time you have the opportunity to better yourself by trying something new, take it. You may hear a voice inside telling you, "You can't!" or "Don't bother!" That's your threshold guardian. Push past it, seize the day, and become stronger because of it.

WRITING TIP Small challenges faced by your hero will help him or her develop character and strength (kind of like leveling up a character in a video game). Think of a challenge your hero will face as he or she takes a first step out of the Ordinary World. How will the unknown world that your hero enters be different from the Ordinary World? How will your hero respond to the challenge?

THE SHADOW

The Joker, Catwoman, the Penguin —all I have to do is mention these villains, and you'll probably think of the superhero who fights against them: Batman. Heroes and villains go hand in hand. The challenges that heroes face define them, so every hero needs some evil to fight.

In a hero story the main evil or "big baddie" that the hero struggles against is called the **shadow.** The shadow is not some minor obstacle along the hero's journey. It is the ultimate evil, the main antagonist to the hero's quest. Usually the hero will not face the shadow until the end of the journey, but the shadow's presence is felt all along the way.

A shadow is a good metaphor for this type of character because the shadow is often a dark reflection of the hero—meaning the shadow is like a twisted version of the hero. By opposing the hero and reflecting the hero's characteristics darkly, the shadow acts as a mirror that shows us more clearly what is truly heroic about the hero. If you think about it, the villains that Batman fights are actually similar to him in a lot of ways: They all wear costumes, use cool gadgets, have traumatic backstories, and live outside normal society. The difference is that Batman's goal is to help others, while the villains are willing to hurt others for their own gain.

The motivations of the shadow are important to consider. Some shadows do evil things simply for evil's sake, but other shadows have more interesting motivations. These shadows may be fighting for a cause—just like the heroes. The difference is how they go about it: Since shadows do not have the internal Hero Code that heroes do, there is nothing that prevents them from using any means necessary to achieve their goals. In their minds the shadows think they are doing the right thing. They may even believe that they are the heroes of the story! But when you measure their actions against right and wrong, it places them on the wrong side of the line. Think about Cruella de Vil, who is willing to skin 101 Dalmatian puppies, just so she can have a new fur coat. Yikes!

A common motivation for shadow characters is revenge. There may be traumatic events in their **backstory** that have prompted them to seek revenge. A backstory is a series of events that have happened before the start of the current story. Often the backstory is revealed through a **flashback** (when a character remembers or the narrator tells readers about previous events). A good example of this comes from the superhero film *Big Hero 6*. The shadow character in that film is trying to seek revenge over the accidental loss of his daughter. We can sympathize with his heartbreak, but when we see that he is willing to harm others to gain his revenge, we realize that he is a shadow. In *Big Hero 6* the main hero Hiro (good name, huh?) is also seeking revenge for the death of his brother, who was killed at the hands of the shadow. By fighting against the shadow and seeing how far the shadow's thirst for revenge has taken him, Hiro learns that revenge is never the answer. Because the hero and the shadow reflect each other, the audience can see what is truly heroic. Revenge is not a heroic goal.

The shadow's backstory can also reflect the hero's own journey in eerie ways. Maybe the shadow used to be a hero but went astray and stopped making heroic choices. In *Star Wars* Luke Skywalker's shadow is Darth Vader, who turns out to be his father who went to the Dark Side long ago. In this case the shadow character shows what could happen if the hero leaves the heroic path and uses his power for evil ends.

In all of the examples so far the shadow has been an actual character in the story, but the shadow is not limited to that role: The shadow can be whatever problem the hero struggles against. It could be a natural disaster (a flood, a storm, an earthquake) or maybe a problem in the world (poverty, hunger, or disease). The shadow could even be part of the hero himself. Think of the Incredible Hulk, the raging green superhero. His biggest struggle is often the fight to control his own destructive rage.

In some hero stories the shadow is redeemed at the end of the journey. A villain can choose to become good. Often heroes will give the shadow characters an option to embrace the good. If the shadow characters refuse this, the hero defeats them. But when the shadow characters accept the hero's offer of mercy, the hero wins a different, more special victory. In *Big Hero 6* Hiro convinces the shadow to let go of his revenge. In the film *Moana* the heroine saves her island by turning the volcanic monster Te Fiti back into the kindly nature goddess she once was.

Whatever form the shadow takes in a hero story, the shadow's presence is often what causes the hero to begin the journey in the first place. The Call to Adventure can be a response to the shadow threatening the hero's world in some way. Often the shadow seems too big and too powerful for the hero to conquer, but this is why we love stories: The hero will have all the courage and skill to emerge victorious.

Through facing the shadow, the hero will conquer the evil within as well.

- Can you think of a particularly mean and nasty shadow that a hero has to face?
- Can you think of a shadow and a hero that resemble and "reflect" each other?
- Can you think of a hero story where the shadow is not another character but a problem that the hero must overcome?

YOUR JOURNEY I wish shadows existed only in stories, but, unfortunately, the real world is filled with evil as well. Sometimes it seems that these real-life shadows are too many and too powerful to overcome. But as stories remind us, no matter how big the giant is, if we face it down bravely, the giant will fall. Just because your shadows exist in the real world, doesn't mean they can't be conquered. Stories take us out of the real world temporarily to remind us of the truth: There is still good in the world, and good will overcome evil.

Shadow characters teach us another important lesson. In your own life you cannot overcome evil with evil. You must overcome evil with good. Just because you feel like you have a good reason to do something hurtful, doesn't mean you should. Consider your choices. Do they violate your inner Hero Code? If you are motivated by anger, greed, or hate, your actions are going to be villainous and shadowy, rather than heroic. And that dark path is not one we want to walk.

WRITING TIP It's true that good villains often make good stories. Think about what kind of shadow your story will have. How will the shadow character be a dark reflection of the hero? What is your shadow's motive for the evil he or she is committing? Does your shadow have a backstory? You may choose to write a story that does not have an actual character who is the shadow, but there must always be a problem to solve. No problem; no story.

THE ROAD OF TRIALS: THE QUEST OF TESTS

Journeys are moving from place to place—but not without a few problems. Have you ever gone on a long trip with your family or friends? Maybe you went by car and somehow got lost along the way. Maybe you went by plane and lost the luggage. Maybe you navigated perfectly, but everyone began to argue and fight halfway through the trip. In every

journey there are always obstacles—flat tires, detours, and potholes. The journey that the hero goes on is sometimes called **The Road of Trials** because the hero must face many obstacles (or trials or tests) one after another.

If you imagined your favorite story as a journey and drew out each event that happened like a roadmap, you would see that the hero of that story went from problem to problem. Once one problem was solved, another one appeared. But since the story is a journey, each problem solved was progress: The hero was one step closer to the goal. Rather than defeating the hero, this constant stream of problems actually made the hero stronger. For example, in the film *Hercules* the strongman hero Hercules must face one monster after another—even battling a many-headed monster called the Hydra that can sprout more heads when one is cut off. This is based on the original Greek myth, where Hercules has to complete twelve tasks (called the Twelve Labors).

Since each new task poses a different challenge for Hercules, he must face each new obstacle differently. He can defeat one monster using his bows and arrows. Another monster is impervious to arrows, so he has to wrestle it into submission. Some of his tasks aren't monsters at all. They're problem-solving situations where he has to use his brains, instead of his brawn. Since each task requires him to use a different skill, he becomes stronger and stronger (mentally and physically) because of the challenges he faces.

The Road of Trials is tough, and there's often an "easy road" that most heroes are tempted to take. But this easy road violates the Hero Code within them. (Shadows are the ones who prefer the easy road.) In the film *Hercules* the villain Hades tempts Hercules to take the easy way out—to be a superficial hero—but in the end

Hercules learns that true sacrifice is necessary for true heroes.

As tough as it can be, the Road of Trials is all-important because it shapes the hero. Heroes can begin their journeys timid and afraid, but somewhere along the way they find their courage. For example, in *The Hobbit* Bilbo, the scaredy-cat hobbit who did not want to leave his home, faces down giant spiders, hobbit-eating trolls, and murderous goblins. Each obstacle helps him find his courage. By the end of the journey, he has built up enough bravery to face down his strongest foe: a fire-breathing dragon.

This change in the hero, brought about by the journey itself, is why many storytellers say, "The journey is the treasure." Most heroes think that the goal of the journey is the most important thing: They can't wait to reach the end, defeat the shadow, and win the treasure they're seeking. They're missing the point. Whatever treasure the heroes are seeking is not as valuable as the wisdom gained along the way. In his story Bilbo and his dwarf companions challenge the dragon to win the dragon's horde of gold—and they do. But the gold is of little consequence to Bilbo. His Road of Trials has changed him forever. Gold may be precious, but wisdom gained along the way is invaluable.

- Think of your favorite hero story. What challenges does the hero have to face?
- How do the obstacles challenge the hero in different ways?
- What strengths does the hero gain by confronting these obstacles?
- Does the hero ever try to take the "easy road"?

YOUR JOURNEY When we encounter problems in life, it is never fun. We don't automatically think, "Another problem! Great! I bet this will help me grow in some way!" But it's true. Like a hero going on a quest, the further we travel and the more obstacles we overcome, the stronger we become. At each stage of our journey we become stronger than we were before. You can picture your life like a map. Each victory is another step that makes you stronger.

A lot of people think that they will only be happy when they reach a certain goal—maybe they want to be taller or older or on the varsity team. They are so fixated on some "treasure" ahead that they don't appreciate the stage of life that they are in. Remember: The journey is the treasure. Enjoy every step along the way.

WRITING TIP Well-written characters change throughout the course of the story. Boring characters do not. As you write your own hero story, think about the ways that your hero's journey is going to change him or her. Each trial or obstacle should present your hero with a different challenge than those faced before and teach the hero a different lesson. Then by the end of the journey your hero will have been changed by these trials. It's up to you to decide how.

ALLIES AND ENEMIES

Teamwork is important—even for heroes. No matter how powerful they are, they cannot accomplish their quest alone. They need allies to assist and help them when the going gets rough.

Allies or companions who accompany the hero are an important part of every hero's journey. Where would Harry Potter be without

Ron and Hermione? Or Luke Skywalker without Han Solo, Princess Leia, and Chewbacca the Wookiee (not to mention R2-D2 and C3PO)? Robin Hood sure couldn't get much *robbin'* done without his merry men.

In Greek mythology there is an ultimate hero team—kind of an ancient Greek Avengers—made up of the most famous Greek heroes. They band together to sail across the seas in search of a legendary artifact called the Golden Fleece. Teamwork is necessary because none of the heroes is powerful enough to do it alone.

"Choose your friends wisely" is great advice for everyone but especially for heroes. Not every character the hero will meet can be trusted, and deciding whom to trust is vital to a hero's success. The beautiful kingdom of Camelot was destroyed when King Arthur trusted people he shouldn't have. The best allies for heroes are those who share their heroic nature, who operate off the same Hero Code. In fact, that's one function that allies serve in the story: They magnify and multiply the heroic traits that the hero already has. If allies do not share the hero's code, they will only lead the hero astray.

Some allies are **animal companions**, hero-support from the animal kingdom. How many heroes rely on their trusty steeds? And when is the last time you saw a fairytale princess without some animal friends tagging along? Cinderella needs those mice! On top of the support they give the hero, these animal companions symbolize the fact that the forces of nature are on the hero's side. In *The Lord of the Rings* even the trees themselves decide to fight alongside the heroes.

Other allies are **loyal retainers**, faithful servants to the hero. Batman trusts very few people with his true identity, but he could not be Batman without the help of his devoted butler Alfred, who knows all his secrets. The loyal retainer's goodness and willingness to help reinforces the hero's dedication to his cause.

Most allies are capable and helpful to the heroes, but have you ever seen an ally who was more of a bumbling fool—the type of character that couldn't do anything right to the point that it was funny? This type of ally called a **trickster,** serves a slightly different purpose: to make the story funnier. In her hero story Mulan could have achieved her quest without the inclusion of a miniature dragon named Mushu, but he is there to give the story some comic relief or material to make it less serious. Some tricksters aren't really helpful at all, and it's hard to even call them allies. The Cheshire Cat in *Alice in Wonderland* can do amusing things like disappearing one stripe at a time and literally standing on his head, but he never truly assists Alice on her journey or seems to care that she's lost in a strange world. In *The*

Wizard of Oz the Wizard of Oz himself, the one whom Dorothy travels so far to meet, is not even really a wizard at all. He's a conman, who has been duping the citizens of Oz! Talk about a trickster!

When an ally is less than helpful to the hero, it's time to view them suspiciously. Sometimes there are characters pretending to be allies but in truth are anything but. They are dark allies or a character type called a **shapeshifter.** This doesn't mean that shapeshifters literally change shape (although they definitely could). It means that their allegiances are not clear. Are they working for the good guys or the bad guys? Shapeshifters may change sides halfway through the story or reveal that they're really not on either side—only looking out for themselves. In Norse mythology the ultimate shapeshifter

is Loki, who betrays the Norse gods as often as he helps them. (His sneaky, two-faced nature carried over into the Marvel movie version of character as well.) Gollum, a muttering, scrawny creature in *The Lord of the Rings,* is constantly warring with himself—will he work for good or for evil? In the end only one side can win out. This makes shapeshifters very dangerous.

An ally could just as easily be a **love interest** for the hero as well. Most princess stories seem to have a Prince Charming somewhere in the mix. But beware: Love interests who are really trying to lead the hero astray are called **temptresses** (or tempters if they're male), and they're really shapeshifters in disguise. Prince Hans from *Frozen,* who presents himself as a love interest for Anna, turns out to be the villain. Megara from the Disney version of *Hercules* pulls a similar move but chooses to be on the side of good by the end. Although this type of character switcheroo can be frustrating, it keeps the story interesting and builds suspense.

Enemies (or characters that oppose the hero) will definitely pop up along the journey as well—much more often than allies. In fact, it might seem like the story has an endless stream of enemies—all with the same goal: to stop the hero. Think of poor Mario the plumber, who was first sucked down into Mushroomland through a sewer pipe. His enemies come in all shapes and sizes: bucktoothed mushrooms, piranha plants, and winged turtles—not to mention King Koopa's bratty children. Yet overcoming these enemies is what makes Mario heroic (and keeps us cheering him on time and time again).

Some enemies are called **creatures of nightmare** because they're grotesque and frightening monsters like werewolves, dementors, goblins, or winged monkeys—the kind of thing you'd see in a bad dream. Not all nightmare creatures are ugly on the outside though. Some are sneakier—devils disguised as angels of light. They may work directly for the shadow or simply be working toward their own evil ends, but they pose formidable obstacles for the heroes.

I mentioned the *Super Mario* game series earlier for a reason. The process of the hero overcoming these enemies along the Road of Trials works something like a video game. The hero defeats enemies, receives special items in return, and grows stronger with the experience he's gained from the victory. In fact, defeating these smaller enemies and tests is what eventually prepares heroes to face the shadow at the end of the journey. If heroes were to face the shadow at the beginning, without experiencing enemies, they would be doomed to failure. (If Mario warped directly to King Koopa, he would be "down the drain.") So by walking the Road of Trials, the hero, assisted by allies and tested by enemies, arrives at the final challenge fully prepared.

- Can you think of a trickster ally in a hero story?
- Can you think of a shapeshifter character, one who maybe changes sides in the story?
- Can you think of a creature of nightmare character?

YOUR JOURNEY Just like the allies that heroes choose show their character, the friends that you choose define your character as well. An old-timer once said, "Skunks only run with other skunks," meaning the company you choose says a lot about you. Benjamin Franklin put it more eloquently: "Those who lie down with dogs will rise up with fleas." If you pick the wrong friends, you will also pick up their bad habits. Choose friends who will build you up and make you better—not bring you down and lead you astray.

There may come a time in your life when only the support of a good friend will get you through.

Just like in hero stories it's tough to know whom to trust. Choose friends who share the same Hero Code as you. This will lead you all down the same path.

Also beware of shapeshifters. There are many people in life who seem good or look good, but in reality they intend to harm or use you. Watch for the warning signs that friends are not true friends. A true friend will not lead you astray or ask you to violate your Hero Code.

WRITING TIP The allies that you give your hero add so much to the story. Funny trickster allies add humor to the story. Shapeshifters add suspense: Are they good, or are they bad? Will they end up betraying the hero? Will they end up becoming heroic themselves? Just as important as the allies are the enemies that your hero must face. How do they challenge the hero in different ways?

THE SUPREME ORDEAL:

APPROACHING THE INMOST CAVE

Caves are frightening places. If you don't believe me, go deep into one and turn out your flashlight. In total darkness your imagination will start to play tricks on you! What kind of sharptoothed creature is lurking invisibly in the darkness? That's why **Approaching the Inmost Cave** is the perfect description for the most intense part of the Hero's Journey. This is where the hero finally reaches the home of the shadow. Most shadows have some kind of lair that is intimidating. (In the oldest stories it was literally a cave.) In modern stories it might be a fortress, a dark land, or a Death Star space station. A lot of questions accompany this stage: What will the hero find there? How will the hero overcome the shadow? Will the hero succeed or fail?

Fortunately for heroes, their journeys have prepared them for this moment. The mentor has given them training, their talisman has supplied them with skill, their allies have encouraged them along the way, and their Road of Trials has strengthened them to the point where they are prepared to face the ultimate test. This step is also known as **The Supreme Ordeal** (not because it comes with all the toppings), but because it is the most challenging thing the hero has faced or will face in the story. Think about when Simba finally returns to Pride Rock to face his evil uncle, Scar. There are dark clouds hanging overhead and flashes of lightning in the sky. The plains around Pride Rock even catch on fire. It's the ultimate showdown between good and evil!

All of the hero's tests along the way have been preparation for this moment, but that doesn't mean the shadow is just going to lie down and submit. Just the opposite! This is a chance for the shadow to show its full, terrifying power. In *The Little Mermaid* Ursula the sea witch grows to an enormous size—big enough to smash a ship. In *Sleeping Beauty* the already-freaky evil fairy Maleficent turns herself into a fire-breathing dragon. In *Aladdin* Jafar the vizier turns himself into a giant snake. See

the trend? Facing off against the shadow is intimidating business!

Yet, even faced with this type of nightmare, heroes respond with courage. Facing the shadow will require heroes to reach deeper into themselves than they ever have before. During the epic struggle between hero and shadow, it may even seem that the hero has been defeated. But their Hero Code will not allow them to quit. Many heroes have been down for the count only to rise again at the last minute. In *Batman Begins* as Batman faces his greatest obstacle, he hears the words of Alfred, his faithful butler, echo in his mind: "Why do we fall, sir? So that we can learn to pick ourselves up." Then the Dark Knight rises once again.

Although the struggle with the shadow is most epic, the hero *never* fights evil with evil. That would not do. Any heroes that use evil to overcome the shadow will become the shadow themselves. As the characters in *The Lord of the Rings* learn, the evil ring of power cannot be used to conquer their enemies, or its power will claim them in the process.

A hero will remain loyal to the Hero Code even it means death. Self-sacrificing heroes are the most inspirational of them all. Yet as Aslan the lion proves in *The Lion, the Witch, and the Wardrobe,* sometimes a hero must die in the name of his cause in order to be reborn even more powerful than before.

In many stories the shadow is so in tune with evil that it preys on all the fears of the hero. So in order for heroes to defeat the shadow, they must defeat a part of themselves. They must give up something that they've been clinging to. They must overcome their fear or let go of their thirst for revenge. In *The Lion King* Scar preys on Simba's guilt over the death of his father, Mufasa. Simba must overcome these emotions before he can take down Scar.

Although the struggle between the hero and the shadow will involve a few cliffhangers (sometimes literally), the bravery of the hero eventually defeats the shadow. How the shadow responds to this defeat varies from story to story. Sometimes the hero offers the shadow mercy because of that inner Hero Code. Sometimes the shadow refuses this offer—only to be destroyed. How many cliffhanging villains have fallen to their deaths because they would not accept the hero's outstretched hand? Other times the defeated shadow takes the offered mercy and becomes a force for good. With the shadow defeated and the Inmost Cave faced, it may seem that the hero's journey is over, but there is still more to come.

- Can you think of an epic hero vs. shadow showdown?
- At some point during the fight does it seem like the shadow has won?
- How does the shadow respond to its defeat at the hands of the hero?
- Does the hero offer the shadow mercy?
- In the end is the shadow destroyed?

YOUR JOURNEY Facing the shadow will look different in everyone's life because we all have different struggles that are personal to us. Your fears might be different from someone else's—but no less frightening. Just like a villain's lair is intimidating and foreboding, so our shadows appear to us. Facing our shadows is important though. To do this, just like heroes, we will have to reach deeper inside ourselves than we have ever reached before. At times it may seem that we have been defeated, but if we continue to rise and oppose the shadow, we will be victorious. Walking away from our problems will only end in fear and misery.

When our shadows in life are other people, it's forgiveness and mercy—not hatred and revenge—that are the tools of a hero. As Abraham Lincoln said, "Do I not destroy my enemy when I make him my friend?" When defeating the shadow, heroes first offer the outstretched hand of mercy.

WRITING TIP An epic showdown between the hero and the shadow will form the climax of your story. Think about where it will take place. Will your shadow have an especially frightening lair? Will the shadow reveal its true power? Will there be a point where it seems like the hero has lost? Adding a bit of suspense into the struggle will intrigue your readers and keep them turning pages. This is the moment that the whole quest has been building toward, so make it as exciting as possible!

RESTORING THE WORLD

The villain, who had been clinging desperately to the edge of the building, does not take the superhero's outstretched hand and plummets down to his death. Game over (for him anyway). The Supreme Ordeal has ended, the climax has passed, but the story continues. There is still more to the Hero's Journey.

Standing in the aftermath of the shadow's defeat, heroes have their moment of victory. They pause—giving them a chance to realize how much they have changed over the course of their journey. Their adventures have made them much more powerful and wiser than before. In this stage of the story called **Rebirth**, some heroes even undergo an outward change. Ariel the mermaid becomes a human for good. Other heroes become the king or queen of their kingdom or receive some other special title or office. At the end of his story Hercules wins the chance to become one of the gods. For some heroes this rebirth is more of an internal change: Simba is finally ready to accept his true position as the Lion King. Luke Skywalker is finally ready to become a Jedi knight.

Usually some prize or reward motivated the hero's journey in the first place, and now it is time to claim this prize. Was it a magical object? A mighty weapon? A secret access code? The rescue of another character? At this point heroes are allowed to claim the reward they sought, which is a stage called **Reward** or **Seizing the Sword**.

In some stories the reward does not achieve what the heroes hoped it would. For example, the Greek heroes who team up to find the Golden Fleece do not end up using it for its intended purpose. King Arthur's knights who seek the Holy Grail finally realize that it does not give them the type of eternal life they are seeking. Dorothy travels all the way across the Land of Oz to meet the Wizard of Oz, only to find out that her ruby slippers had the power to take her home all along. In these instances the heroes must realize that the real reward was the journey itself. (The audience must realize that, too, or they might feel ripped off.)

In the original Greek myth Hercules, after winning the chance to become one of the gods, ascends to Mount Olympus and does just that. But in the Disney film version of the same story Hercules instead chooses to give up his immortality and live a mortal life with his one true love. Although the two versions of the stories end differently—one in which the hero claims the reward and the other where the hero gives up the reward—both endings are satisfying.

With the shadow defeated and the reward claimed, all that is left for the hero to do is to return home. Yet this return journey is not always simple and could have its own lesser challenges to conquer. After slaying Medusa, Perseus returns home but stops along the way to save a beautiful princess from a sea serpent. It's nothing compared to killing Medusa, but it's still an adventure! These post-shadow adventures are always lesser in scope with smaller stakes. Sometimes the hero receives a magical flight back home—skipping any obstacles that might occur along the way. In the film *The Wizard of Oz* Dorothy simply flies home through the use of her ruby slippers. But in the original book she has a few more adventures before arriving back in Kansas.

Once heroes return home to the Ordinary World, their efforts have solved the problem that originally spurred them to accept the Call to Adventure in the first place. This stage is called **Restoring the World** because the hero has saved the day—often saving their world from destruction. Now the hero is celebrated and thanked by the same people who maybe once considered the hero to be an outcast. Saving the whole world isn't for every hero though. Some heroes just save a piece of their smaller world—like when Marlin finds his son Nemo. Even if the stakes seem smaller, they are just as important to the hero.

With the hero home again the story has come full circle. The task that seemed impossible has been completed, and the hero can reflect on the journey and its meaning. As Samwise Gamgee, Frodo's faithful ally in *The Lord of the Rings,* tells his friend, "It's like in the great stories, Mr. Frodo—the ones that really mattered. Full of darkness and danger they were. And sometimes you didn't want to know the end. Because how could the end be happy? How could the world go back to the way it was when so much bad had happened? But in the end, it's only a passing thing, this shadow. Even darkness must pass. A new day will come. And when the sun shines it will shine out the clearer. Those were the stories that stayed with you—that meant something—even if you were too small to understand why."

Back in the Ordinary World, heroes can truly realize how much they have grown. They are not the same people that they were at the beginning of the journey. As Alice reflects on her adventures in Wonderland, she says, "It's no use going back to yesterday. I was a different person then." This might be bittersweet: If heroes did not feel out of place in the Ordinary World before, they might now. Their home seems smaller and simpler—not as satisfying as before. They might say to themselves, "I think I'm quite ready for another adventure."

True heroes will not sit at home for long. Some of them become mentors for the next generation of heroes. Some aren't done being heroes themselves. Soon another adventure will come calling, and like before they will rise to the challenge.

- Can you think of a way that a hero "restores the world" at the end of his or her journey?
- What reward does that hero receive at the end of the journey?
- Do the people in the Ordinary World treat the hero differently now?
- How has the hero changed along the course of the journey? Has the hero experienced "rebirth"?

YOUR JOURNEY The real world is full of problems, and we need real-life heroes now more than ever. Use the heroes of stories as your inspiration. How can you make the world a better place? What is a problem you see in the world that you could confront? What quest would you undertake if you knew you couldn't fail? Listen to your Hero Code inside. If you follow your Call to Adventure, you just might save the world.

WRITING TIP What lesson or lessons has your hero learned throughout the journey? Heroes who don't learn something or change in some way are less interesting than ones who do. Resolving all the loose ends is the story's most satisfying part for most readers. They want to see how the hero has solved the problem that was created at the beginning. "And they lived happily ever after" is a cliché ending, but it sums up what readers want to hear. They want to know that the world is safe and sound once again—at least for now.

JOURNEY'S END

So the journey of this book is over, but as an old song says, "Every new beginning comes from some other beginning's end." Now that you know the building blocks that go into the Hero's Journey, you will be able to create one yourself. Armed with the lessons of this pattern, you can also have the courage to be a hero in your own life. In the real world you do not get to play a supporting role. You must be the hero of your own life. You must act. Listen to your Hero Code. Accept the Call to Adventure. Discover your talisman. Seek out mentors and allies to help along the way. Don't be discouraged by threshold guardians and enemies. Face your shadow, restore the world, and make it a better place—because that's what heroes do. Enjoy the journey!

The Road goes ever on and on
Down from the door where it began.
Now far ahead the Road has gone,
And I must follow, if I can,
Pursuing it with eager feet,
Until it joins some larger way
Where many paths and errands meet.
And whither then? I cannot say.

RECOMMENDED HERO STORY READING

The Hobbit by J.R.R. Tolkien

The Lord of the Rings by J.R.R. Tolkien

The Chronicles of Narnia by C.S. Lewis

The Prydain Chronicles by Lloyd Alexander

A Wizard of Earthsea by Ursula K. Le Guin

King Arthur and His Knights of the Round Table by Roger Lancelyn Green

Tales of the Greek Heroes by Roger Lancelyn Green

The Adventures of Robin Hood by Roger Lancelyn Green

The Phantom Tollbooth by Norton Juster

Matilda by Roald Dahl

The Squires' Tales by Gerald Morris

Redwall by Brian Jacques

GRAPHIC NOVEL HERO STORIES

Bone: The Complete Cartoon Epic by Jeff Smith

Uncle Scrooge Comics by Carl Barks and Don Rosa

The Adventures of Tintin by Hergé

REFERENCES

Campbell, Joseph. *The Hero with a Thousand Faces.* Novato: New World Library, 2008.

Volger, Chris. *The Writer's Journey.* Saline: McNaughton and Gunn, Inc., 2007.

ABOUT THE AUTHOR

Zachary Hamby is an English teacher in rural Missouri. Being a lifelong fan of hero stories, he loves teaching young people about heroes both ancient and modern. He is the author of the *Reaching Olympus* and *Mythology for Teens* textbook series, which he also illustrated. He resides in the Ozarks with his wife, Rachel (also an English teacher), and their two children. For more information about Zachary visit his website **www.creativeenglishteacher.com** or contact him by email at **hambypublishing@gmail.com**

Made in the USA
Las Vegas, NV
18 March 2022